REALMS OF ART

General Editor: PROFESSOR D. TALBOT RICE

STAINED GLASS WINDOWS

VICTOR BEYER

Edited by
DAVID TALBOT RICE

Translated by
M. von HERZFELD *and* R. GAZE

OLIVER & BOYD
EDINBURGH AND LONDON

OLIVER AND BOYD LTD
Tweeddale Court
Edinburgh 1

39a Welbeck Street
London W.1

Das Grosse Erbe
A translation of *Offenbarung der Farbe*
published by Buch-Kunstverlag, Ettal

First English Edition 1964

Plates printed by H. Weixler, Oberammergau
Text printed in Great Britain by Morrison & Gibb Ltd, London and Edinburgh

INTRODUCTION

In Plato's philosophy truth and beauty were one, and in the Middle Ages theologians enlarged upon this idea by saying that, as beauty cannot be perceived without light, it is to light that truth owes its radiance and its power. They therefore regarded light as a gift from God, the "divine sun" as Suger (1081–1151), the abbot of Saint Denis, called it.

This concept of light was the mainspring of all medieval art, in which man expressed his thoughts and emotions; it is particularly applicable, however, to the art of stained glass, of which light must be considered an integral part. The relationship between light and stained glass was indeed compared to that between soul and body, and there thus seemed to be a mystical link between glass (a substance of this world) and light (which comes from the ether), which cannot be seized by human hands, and yet permeates everything.

This mystical relationship between glass and light was an essential element in medieval ways of thought. Glass is the product of a process in which quartz-sand, potash or sodium, iron, manganese, copper, etc.—that is terrestial elements—are converted by fire into a new substance, itself mystically connected with the divine light. One could thus see in this process a symbol of the relation between things terrestial and things eternal, the truth of which was experienced wherever stained glass glistened in the twilight interior of a church. This transcendental

5

effect was further intensified by the appeal of colour, thanks to the various psychological and physiological reflexes produced by it, so that it was difficult to distinguish between what belonged to heaven and what to earth.

It was this experience which led the early fathers of the church, the first authors of Christendom, to extol in lyrical terms the splendour of the brilliant effects produced by glass and light in association. In the fourth century for instance, when the Church had achieved a more settled position under Constantine, Prudentius wrote:

"In the round arches of the windows in the basilica shone glass in colours without number, resplendent like a field in spring."

IN the Middle Ages man looked upon the churches as symbols of the heavenly Jerusalem, as it was described in the Revelation of St. John, 21, 9–21. This idea was symbolised particularly in Hagia Sophia at Constantinople, where the golden mosaic of the dome, shining in the light which poured in through the windows of the drum, seemed to represent the vault of heaven. The same conception seems to characterise the dazzling blue of the mosaics of the mausoleum of Galla Placidia at Ravenna, while in western Europe the high and radiant windows of Gothic churches exercise the same effect.

The medieval idea of salvation allowed for another symbolic interpretation of the relationship between light and glass, which St. Bernard of Clairvaux (1090–1153) described:

> "As the glorious sun penetrates glass without breaking it . . . so the Word of God, the light of the Father, passes through the body of the Virgin, and then leaves it without undergoing any change."

In view of this it is not surprising that, owing to its quasi-transcendental character, the art of stained glass came to be regarded as the most truly Christian of all the arts.

In the Renaissance stained glass retained its importance as an integral part of architecture, nor did the harmony of its colours deteriorate; but its character changed, and it gradually lost the power to convince because the religious significance of the themes of its subject matter were less deeply felt by the artists. It was secularised, in accordance with the new classical taste, and greater emphasis came to be laid upon ornamentation than upon any spiritual theme.

In the seventeenth century a number of immense windows were still erected, but they were as often as not transparent, devoid of colour and therefore lacking in the quality of mysticism, and this trend was accentuated in the eighteenth century, the century of "enlightenment." A characteristic example of the new attitude towards this art is the experience of Daniel Danneker of Strasbourg, who wrote to the king, calling himself "the rediscoverer of stained glass painting"; but the king in his reply told him that no one was interested in this art any longer, as the dimming of light was of no use whatsoever for devotion, either in the church or in the home.

A true understanding of stained glass was not recaptured until recently, when there has been a new movement towards the irrational and magical, and a new relationship to divine mysteries has developed. This changed attitude is exemplified in the works of such modern artists as Rouault, Matisse, Léger, Bazaine, or Chagall, and in Germany by Duelberg, Meistermann, and others.

The shape and size of stained glass windows has always depended on the style of the architecture which provided the frame for them. The exact period when the making of stained glass was invented is unknown. Disks of glass and the insertion of pieces of glass into other material were certainly known in early Antiquity and in early Moslem times.[1] Fragments of stucco covered with painted glazing, so-called stucco-transennae, were for instance found in Jericho. But it is difficult to distinguish between the initial stages of stained glass and work in mosaic; the only fairly reliable information we have comes from literary tradition, which mentions stained glass either in the form of ornamental disks or as a means of illustrating a given theme.

The nature of the architectural framework of the windows is known to us only from the Carolingian era, and only with the early Romanesque age do we come to know anything in real detail. The windows then consisted of narrow, round arches, cut deep and slantwise into the wall and filled with sparkling glass, the magical fascination of which may be compared to that of the precious stones in the work of the contemporary goldsmiths, like the glorious Madonna of the Ottonian period at Essen or the strange figure of St. Foy at Conques in France—though admittedly (as St. Bernard feared) there was in such things a danger to Christian piety.

Examples of stained glass from these earliest days are provided by fragments of a head from Lorsch in Hesse, now in the museum at Darmstadt, an impressive head of Christ from Wissembourg in Alsace, now in the Frauenhaus Museum at Strasbourg,[2] and the original and enigmatic roundel with a cross from Séry-les-Mézières (Aisne), which may possibly be older than either of the others, and date perhaps from the ninth century.[3] The heyday of Romanesque stained glass did not come till the twelfth century, when windows with small medallions—as well as others with rows of figures—became usual, like those with the prophets in Augsburg,[4] dating from the first half of the century, or those in Strasbourg with rows of prophets, emperors, and the kings of the Holy Roman Empire, dating from the end of the twelfth century.[5]

In the Gothic period the surface area of the walls as well as the mass of the masonry in the churches was reduced in a marvellous new system of equilibrium, the weight of the walls being taken by the main keystones, and which thereby led to a consistent transference of stress with the help of relieving walls and flying buttresses, and to the reduction as far as was possible of the actual wall space, as can be seen in the delightful Sainte Chapelle at Paris (consecrated in 1248) or the chancel of Saint Etienne at Beauvais, while in Germany the churches

9

and cathedrals of Aachen, Cologne, Regensburg, Erfurt, Esslingen, Wimpfen, Stendal, and many others serve as examples. In these churches huge windows were built almost like walls of glass, and this large-scale use of stained glass, which told stories in vivid colours, formed the Gothic equivalent of the wall paintings of the Romanesque age.

The pictures that glowed in the windows not only gratified the delight taken by medieval man in stories, but also served to evoke devout feelings in him. Events of the Bible story or from legends of the saints were probably reproduced in glass on a large scale for the first time in the first half of the twelfth century under the patronage of Abbot Suger of Saint Denis. Viewed as a whole, these vast high windows somewhat resembled hanging tapestries. The panes of glass of which they were composed were assembled systematically in ornamental designs as at Chartres or Bourges, and the metal rods served a double purpose— both to fasten the panes and to determine the pattern of the window. Sometimes the panes were put together quite simply side by side or in vertical rows, but then painted architectural details, such as canopies, were usually added, as for instance at Amelungsborn near Brunswick.[6] Or again, especially in windows with symbolic themes, glass medallions were placed one above the other, and linked by painted festoons or by a background made up of geometrical designs.

In the fourteenth century in particular an important role was played by stained glass adorned with architectural motifs, which served to complement those formed by the real architecture and so considerably increased the effect. Efforts in this direction were not always successful, however, for in some instances strangely fantastic images were produced, as for example in St. Catherine's Chapel in the minster at Strasbourg (dating from about 1350),[7] or on the west wall of the monastery church at Altenberg near Cologne in the late fourteenth century,[8] or again at Vienna, about 1400.[9]

Originally this painted architecture was restricted to pictures on a single plane, but soon perspective became popular, and towards the end of the century, obviously under the influence of the Italian *trecento*, this led to a playful use of patterns, sometimes of architectural details,[10] and sometimes formed of cubes. In this context must be mentioned the foliage and branch frames on stained glass from the workshop of Peter Hemmel von Andlau, a glass-painter at Strasbourg in the second half of the fifteenth century,[11] as well as the columns which towards the end of the Middle Ages were frequently painted on the windows to serve as frames for the pictures. Some of the columns depicted had deep flutings, others were surrounded by ribbons; they were to be found as early as in the fifteenth century in Munich in the Liebfrauenkirche (Church of Our Lady), and later in many Renaissance windows and groups of disks.

With the Renaissance came a tendency to transgress the limits of the windowpanes with pictures of large figures or perspective landscapes, extended even further by festoons. There are plenty of examples of this tendency in every country, but especially in Italy, where they came into use very early, as there the Renaissance style developed straight from the classical foundations. They also occurred, however, in the Low Countries, especially in work from the studio of the brothers Crabeth;[12] today, however, hardly any stained glass windows have survived in that area.

As a result of this use of perspective, and particularly thanks to the stressing of the pictorial element—a trend which was influenced by contemporary engravings and paintings—the art of stained glass gradually came to renounce its chief characteristic, the use that it made of the elemental power of light and colour, although some masterpieces were produced even in the sixteenth and seventeenth centuries. But in the eighteenth century the making of coloured glass was almost entirely abandoned in favour of white glass with ornamental golden borders, as can be seen for example in the chapel at Versailles.[13] The nineteenth century, with its imitation of Romanesque, Gothic, and Renaissance art, reintroduced bright colours into the churches, but often in crude shades and in a forced or sentimental manner; this endeavour to recreate history proved a mistake, because although the Romantic Movement was satisfied, the art of stained glass suffered.

It is only modern glass-painting that has re-discovered the essential character of the earlier art; like much other modern painting it has given up photographic reproduction, preferring a simpler and more austere technique, which is in keeping with the character of the material. A comparable situation is to be found, however, in the art of tapestry, which shares the same problems. With Georges Rouault and Jean Lurcat both arts have returned to the sources of their styles.

W E have briefly discussed the general history of stained glass windows and their designs, but it is important to bear in mind that the effect achieved by stained glass is chiefly dependent on the colours, while their gradation and combination offers further possibilities to the artist. It is in this combination of design with colour that the mysterious nature of light is revealed.

The choice of colours has varied with the different epochs, countries, and psychological trends. In France in the earlier years there was a predilection for harmonising red and blue, as for instance in the rose windows at Chartres or in Notre Dame at Paris, whereby, especially in the thirteenth century, a dim purplish, basically mystic, atmosphere was produced in church interiors. This quality became even more marked—it was perhaps almost too purposeful—when the grisaille windows were introduced, for which the Cistercians had a marked preference.[14] There is no finer example of a grisaille window than the so-called Five Sisters window at the end of the north transept in York Minster. In the Rhineland, on the other hand, stress was laid as early as the Romanesque period on the interplay of green and yellow with blue and red, so that the general impression was less restrained and more cheerful. Yet too strict a classification would be a mistake.

In the thirteenth century the colours used were fundamentally stronger in tone than those which prevailed in the fourteenth, when the grisaille method was increasingly employed, together with the use of a sunny silvery yellow, as in the beautiful window at Altenberg. In certain districts, probably linked in some way with each other (such as Thann in Alsace, Vienna, and Erfurt), the most popular colour combination towards the end of the fourteenth century was red, purple, green, and brown, balanced by some patches of white. In the fifteenth century the combinations of colours were generally made still more striking, though their harmony sometimes suffered from over-violent contrasts, especially as the base, against which the pictures stood out, was not treated as a linking device for the work as a whole. Peter Hemmel von Andlau, however, managed to retain harmony in his work, in spite of his use of brilliant and striking colours.[15]

In the Renaissance the colours were distributed over the surface in a new manner: they were not concentrated within the frames provided by the architecture, such as window-panes, or by geometrical designs, but were collected in massive groups alternating with empty fields or with fields partially or lightly coloured, as for instance in the parish church at Landsberg on the Lech, or in the Salvator Church at Munich.[16] Frequently, however, shining architectural decorations were used to balance and support such compositions.

I T is rewarding to observe the development of stained glass not only according to its epochs and styles, but also according to its place of origin. Great differences appear, as glass-painting everywhere was influenced by the prevailing ethos, the attitude of the people, and local tradition—the *genius loci*. But one must beware of generalising, because all medieval artists—and glass-painters in particular—loved to move from workshop to workshop. This is the explanation for the surprising conformity of works far removed from each other: in the thirteenth century, for example, the works in the so-called Saxon-Westphalian jagged style, which are to be found from Mönchen-Gladbach in the Rhineland to Strasbourg, Merseburg, and Naumburg—and even as far away as the upper church of San Francesco at Assisi. The same applies at the end of the fourteenth and the beginning of the fifteenth century to certain works in Austria, like those at St. Stephan's and of Maria am Gestade (St. Mary on the Shore) at Vienna, or in Alsace, as for example in St. Theobald's at Thann, or the cathedral of Erfurt in Thuringia.

France, the true home of the Gothic style, was also that of stained glass, for its great cathedrals of the twelfth and thirteenth centuries were dependent on light pouring in, even at that early date. The decisive impetus to glass-painting was indeed probably given by Suger of Saint Denis, who was assisted by a group of artists coming from various sources. Unfortunately only fragments have survived from these important early windows.[17]

15

These works were, however, not the only ones dating from this early period, as the windows of Séry-les-Mézières were contemporary with them. In the west of France the Romanesque style was responsible for another important group, on which the illuminated manuscripts of the south-west and Limoges exerted a strong influence; its centre was at Le Mans, where the magnificent apostles in the picture of the Ascension of Christ in the minster are remarkably striking.[18] From there the style radiated to Mont-Saint-Michel, Angers, Poitiers, and the Church of the Trinity at Vendôme. Another group had its home in the east, notably in Saint Rémi at Reims and in Châlons-sur-Marne; in style it was closely connected with the art of the goldsmiths of the Maas District, chiefly at Verdun, and of the Rhineland.[19] The late Romanesque stained glass of the Rhineland and the windows in the minster at Strasbourg, dating from about 1200, naturally show similarities with the work of this group.

The fate of the cathedral of Chartres[20] was more fortunate than that of Saint Denis, and Chartres in turn exercised a great influence on the stained glass of Rouen—*Clemens vitrearius carnitensis me fecit* was recorded of glass there—as well as at Amiens and Poitiers; in England, Canterbury and Lincoln also owe a great debt to Chartres.

About 1245, however, a new centre was established with the glass of the Sainte Chapelle and with Notre Dame at Paris,[21] and this style spread to Soissons, Tours, Le Mans, Angers, Amiens, Beauvais, and Clermont-Ferrand. Just before and particularly after the turn of the century a number of local styles developed in France, which were independent of Chartres or Paris; they were to be found in the north at Laon—which was later to influence the style of the great rose window in the cathedral at Lausanne in Switzerland[22]—and in Burgundy, at Sens, Bourges, and Auxerre, as well as at Lyon (which seems to have had connections with Germany), and eventually in the Champagne, at Troyes between Maas and Rhine.[23]

During the centuries when the towns were rising in importance, this regional individuality (which was, however, still to some extent under the influence of some of the courts) gained ground, especially as worldly-mindedness spread everywhere, and art became increasingly dependent on the demands of the donors, whether burghers, nobles, or guilds. In this period more use than ever was made of illuminated manuscripts as models, such as those by Jean Pucelle or by Jacquemart de Hesdin, as for example at Evreux. L. Grodecki has summarised this trend in the following terms:[24]

"The regional schools of the fifteenth century were extremely prolific, in Normandy as well as in the Champagne, in the east, the north and the centre of France; masterpieces were produced for Saint Séverin in Paris, for the side chapels at Bourges, the Sainte Chapelle at Riom and for the episcopal palace at Rouen. In the seventeenth century the art of stained glass declined, but once again shone out before its end in Troyes, Paris and Normandy."

The names of some of the prominent Renaissance artists in stained glass must be mentioned: most important were the brothers Le Prince at Beauvais, Geoffrey Dumonistier and Arnoult of Nimegen in Rouen, Matthieu Bléville at Saint Quentin and Châlons in the Champagne, Jean Lecuyer in Bourges, Arnaut de Moles in Auch in the south-west, and Valentin Busch at Metz.[25]

In Italy, where the Gothic style never became popular, the use of stained glass was more restricted; yet there too some masterpieces are to be found. But there was no architectural foundation for this kind of art, and in addition stained glass passed with little notice amidst the profusion of paintings and frescoes, although it was usually the great artists in these techniques who made the working drawings for the glass, yet they left the actual work to the specialist glass-workers. The most important centre of glass-painting was at Assisi,[26] in the double basilica of San Francesco with its numerous stained glass windows; some of these were made in the traditional Gothic style of the north, while others conformed more to the styles of Giotto or of Simone Martini and Duccio. Both these schools had a decisive influence on the development of stained glass in Italy.[27]

In Or San Michele at Florence the Gothic tradition was upheld with subtlety and understanding, whereas the windows in Santa Croce, placed between sections of painted wall, contain rows of standing figures by Taddeo Gaddi, Maso di Banco, and others. In the apse and in the west rose window of the Church of Santa Maria Novella are works by Andrea di Firenze, 1365–66, Domenico Ghirlandaio, 1490, and Fiorentino, 1492; some are therefore in the Gothic, some in the Renaissance style, while in Santa Maria del Fiore there are windows by Lorenzo Ghiberti, Paolo Ucello, and Andrea del Castagno.[28]

Though the magnificent Sienese School was less rich in stained glass, the large round window in the apse of the cathedral at Siena, with its wonderful radiance, must be noted; it is a work by Duccio. In Orvieto there is a cycle of the life of the Virgin by Lorenzo Maitani.[29] Italian stained glass is characterised by the famous all-round perfection of Italian drawing, the purity of its colours, and their decorative charm.

Although there was an old-established glass industry at Murano, which had flourished with distinction in the fifteenth and sixteenth centuries, Venice[30] nevertheless produced very few stained glass windows. Of these there are some dating from the beginning of the fourteenth century in the church of the Frari, and others, in Renaissance style, in SS. Giovanni e Paolo; these were designed by Mocetto in 1473. There are also some examples of stained glass in San Domenico at Perugia, San Petronio at Bologna, and in Padua and Lombardy, where the era of Italian glass-painting neared its end with the windows in the cathedral at Milan,[31] presented by the various guilds and fraternities. Finally there is some stained glass in the monastery of the Carthusians at Pavia and in the cathedral at Arezzo, where Guglielmo de Marsillat, a Frenchman who came from Rome and Cortona, worked at the beginning of the sixteenth century.[32]

Spanish glass-painting was obviously influenced by France and the Netherlands; there is some particularly fine work in the cathedral at Léon, with its windows built high up in the clerestory, the triforium, and the side aisles.[33] But in Spain stained glass makes a poor showing in comparison with other painting.

In England stained glass developed to a magnificent, almost lyrical bloom during the Middle Ages. In Lincoln, Canterbury, and York it was strongly influenced from France, especially Saint Denis and above all Chartres. The great age of English stained glass started in the twelfth century and declined towards the end of the sixteenth. The largest number of works—as well as the most original ones—date from the fourteenth century, the beginning of the epoch of the perpendicular style; some of them are to be found in small churches such as Arlingham, Deerhurst, Tewkesbury, Fladbury, Norgrove, and Birt Morton—others in cathedrals such as Wells and Gloucester. To the fifteenth century belong some windows of great beauty in a vigorous, sometimes almost violent style: windows at East Harling, Clavering, Ketteringham, and Great Malvern are outstanding. In the fourteenth century in particular there were indisputable connections between the art of glass-painting and other techniques, notably panel and miniature painting. Towards the end of the sixteenth century Flemish influence became noticeable, as in the lovely windows at Fairford or in the

King's College chapel at Cambridge. The strength of the English artists in stained glass lay in their portraiture and in their treatment of heraldic themes in ornamental panes.[34]

Swiss stained glass, though the range is smaller, is nevertheless important: the beautiful row of windows at Königsfelden belongs to the first half of the fourteenth century; there is a most interesting rose window in the cathedral at Lausanne, while the monastery at Wettingen, dating from the thirteenth century, the church at Muenchenbuchsee, and the important chancel of the minster at Bern, dating from the fifteenth century, can boast of several impressive series of windows, influenced from nearby Alsace, the north of France, Germany, and Austria. The stained glass of Königsfelden, which dates from the first half of the fourteenth century, shows a certain affinity with the art of the court of the Habsburgs.[35] Influenced by the architecture of Strasbourg as well as by Italian painting of the *trecento*, its refined style spread not only to Rosenweiler and Niederhaslach in Alsace, and to the Dominican church at Strasbourg, but also further afield to Regensburg, Freiburg im Breisgau, and even to Austria, where it was combined with Bohemian elements.[36]

In Germany, including Alsace, Austria, and the German part of Switzerland, there were fewer centres with pronounced ascendency over others than in France, although the influence of some of them was exercised at fairly great distances. Not that this is easy to assess, for any enquiry into the history of German stained glass is hampered because Germany has lost much of its glass in the course of the centuries. What has survived outside a few centres does not warrant any classification according to schools, though one can distinguish characteristic styles and particular groups and see their relationship to each other.

In the late Romanesque period there was along the Rhine a group of works of a distinctive style, known as the Gerlachus Group, which was somewhat influenced by the art of the goldsmiths of the Maas District and Champagne;[37] to it belong windows dating from about 1200 in the minster of Strasbourg, some pieces of stained glass in the museum at Frankfurt, and the portrait of the glass-painter Gerlachus in the castle at Kapfenberg. A wave of French influence— characterised by a preference for glass medallions, which had been popular in the churches of the friars—spread from Strasbourg and Wissembourg in Alsace to Swabia and to the Lower Rhine, to Wimpfen, Esslingen, Mönchen-Gladbach, and Cologne (as in the Dominicans' windows in the cathedral there).[38] Indeed a direct influence from the north of France, extending from Amiens to Cologne, became noticeable in stained glass as well as in architecture.

Then there was the so-called Saxon-Westphalian Group, in which medallion windows were also popular; it was modelled on the psalter of Aschaffenburg, which had itself been influenced by French miniature painting.[39] This group represented what is known as Romanesque Mannerism, a baroque branch of German Romanesque art, which spread from Strasbourg to Mönchen-Gladbach and Naumburg.

Towards the end of the fourteenth and the beginning of the fifteenth centuries another surprisingly strong group emerged in Vienna, Erfurt, Ulm, Rothenburg on the Tauber, and Thann in Alsace.[40] Its main features were the representation in stained glass of colourful and complicated architecture, such as canopies or buildings with battlements, rounded arches, etc., and the use of black manganese to paint broad lines in strong relief. In Austria[41] examples of this kind of art are to be found in Vienna in the Herzogenkapelle (Dukes' chapel) of the cathedral, and in the church of Maria am Gestade (St. Mary on the Shore); from there this technique spread to the provinces, where there are some beautiful works at Maria Strassengel near Graz, in Ebreichsdorf, at St. Erhard in Styria, and in the chancel of the Cistercian monastery at Viktring in Carinthia.[42]

Immediately after this group another interesting one emerged, which closely linked the Besserer Kapelle of the minster at Ulm[43] with Setting in Lorraine,[44] and with the windows in the chancel of the minster at Bern.[45]

Although lack of space makes it impossible to discuss this in more detail or to enumerate further groups of local styles, mention must be made here of the stained glass from the workshop of Peter Hemmel von Andlau, dating from the second half of the fifteenth century, which exercised some influence even on works of the sixteenth century, and reached from Strasbourg to Lorraine, southern Germany, and Austria.

ANYONE interested in stained glass will wish to learn some details about its technique, especially as it has sometimes been said that the medieval glass-painters used secret methods which are unknown today, for example the technique of producing the lovely shining blue glass of the twelfth century. Of course there are special recipes and tricks of the trade as in all arts and skills, but in general the technique of making stained glass has been well known since the end of the eleventh century, as Theophilus, a monk in a Benedictine monastery near Paderborn, described the process in exact detail in his *Diversarium artium schedula*.[46]

There would be no difficulty about using his recipes today, but the modern glass-maker has acquired a refined technique, and—though this may sound paradoxical—this makes the new glass considerably less impressive than the old. Stained glass comes to life through chance imperfections: light shines irregularly through coarse or uneven glass full of air-bubbles or scars, and this very greatly enhances the effect. Nowadays "faults," that is artificial unevenness and irregularities, are produced intentionally in the industrial process of making glass disks. Though today the basic elements are considerably purer, the product of the modern technique usually compares poorly with medieval stained glass; besides, the Middle Ages had a more profound conception of art and greater creative power.

In the eleventh and twelfth centuries potash derived from wood ash was mixed in fire-resistant tubs in the ratio of two to one with river sand. The light iron oxide of the sand gave the glass a greenish or yellowish tone; the depth of the colour depended on the length of time that the heat was applied. After the thirteenth century natrium was used, but though this refined the process, it deprived the glass of its former hardness. It became possible, however, to obtain thinner glass, which could be cut into pieces of more complicated shapes. This cutting operation was by no means easy, and a great deal of glass was lost in the process. But it led to considerable technical dexterity, for example to such complicated feats as the excision of the eyes from coloured glass figures and the substitution of white glass. This was done with a tool called a grozing iron. Today diamonds are used for this, which cut very sharply—too sharply, in fact, as they make it even more difficult for the newer glass in its network of leads to withstand gusts of wind or the vibrations set up by jet aeroplanes.[47]

There were two methods of making glass disks: in the so-called muff method a sphere of glass was blown with a hollow rod and drawn out into a cylinder; both ends of this were then cut off and the cylinder cut lengthwise and flattened down into a smooth slab. The other method, known as the crown method, consisted in making a hole at only one point of the sphere, and then spinning the rod rapidly until the sphere had flattened out into a kind of bull's-eye roundel with a diameter of approximately fifty centimetres (twenty inches). The latter method produced less regular disks than the former, as the formation of concentric zones and of a nipple in the centre could not be avoided. The varying intensity of the colours corresponded to this unevenness of the glass, and this was put to very skilful use for the modelling of the flesh tints or the garments, and for the shading of the background.

In considering the method by which the colours were applied to and fused with the glass, one must distinguish between pot metal glass and flashed glass.

The former came ready and coloured from the glass-maker, and had been given its colour by the admixture of metallic oxides, such as oxide of cobalt for blue, oxide of manganese for violet, oxide of iron for green or yellow, and oxide of copper for ruby. These colours had become an indivisible element of the glass. There was, however, a drawback to this method, as it made ruby appear almost opaque.

Flashed glass, on the other hand, was made by immersing a sphere of concentrated coloured pot metal glass in molten colourless glass, after which it was blown up further and then treated in the manner described above. This process could also be reversed: a small sphere of colourless glass could be immersed in a coloured liquid and then blown up, but in either way thin layers of colour were produced. Sometimes different colours of glass in liquid form were stirred together to obtain glass disks with fairly thin stripes, and frequently several layers of different colours were made one on top of the other to give particular effects. The advantage of this was that one could gradate shades at will, apply the colours more lightly, and engrave the glass by abrading or rubbing away a layer of colour wherever the design required.

A full-sized working drawing of the picture was then made on a flat wooden board, and the pieces of glass, cut to shape, were laid upon it, with the design showing through; the glass was fastened to the board with small nails, called closing nails. The outlines of the design were then drawn on to the glass with a brush in a dark mixture of pulverised glass and manganese, to which some iron or copper oxide had been mixed at a low melting point; when heated to six hundred degrees centigrade (about eleven hundred degrees Fahrenheit) this mixture fused with the softened pane of glass.

The drawing and the painting were applied to the glass in three layers: first came a thin coat, then a somewhat thicker one to model the picture further, and finally strong lines were drawn to trace the contours.[48] Some special effects were produced, in particular after the fifteenth century, such as a refined modelling by wiping or scraping with a dry brush or some sharp tool, or by cross-hatching as in engravings. Frequently black manganese was laid on the outside of the glass to set off the drawing.[49] After the fifteenth century it became popular to make engravings on flashed glass, usually on red, sometimes on blue glass, while in the Renaissance enamel (i.e. liquid colour) was increasingly used, being applied to parts of the picture with a brush.

When the cold paints had been fired in moderate heat and thereby fused with the glass, and all the glass pieces had been assembled on the working drawing, the next step was to fit the pieces together with cross bars of lead, grooved (in section) like the letter H. These made the picture look more striking, and helped with the composition of the colours as do the black contours in the paintings of the Fauvists, separating the colours to make them look clear and fresh.[50] This network of leads was elastic and withstood gusts of wind, especially when reinforced at the sides by wooden battens. Yet few of the original leads have survived. The nets of the leads were loosened by the continual impact of the wind, while the glass suffered from chemical dissolution as the metals oxidised, so that restorations, replacements, and repairs have continuously had to be carried out throughout the centuries, and only in rare cases has any completely intact stained glass survived from the Middle Ages; even in the best preserved windows new leads have had to be laid over cracks as an added precaution, or as "stop-gaps."

In early stained glass the black manganese frequently flaked off, though occasionally it was the parts protected by it which remained intact, while the uncovered surface suffered from the weather so that the outside of these windows now appears whitish. This was usually due to a faulty application of the black manganese to the glass, and today this poses considerable problems to the restorer. The usual rough method of patching, which replaced damaged pieces with modern glass, or the use of stop-gap leads, not to mention the often inadequately controlled new methods, are all risky operations.[51]

The present industrial age with its mechanical, atmospheric, and chemical processes of decay and dissolution, endangers the treasures of former ages more than ever, and puts stained glass in a well-nigh tragic situation. It is therefore important at least to make its present state known through coloured reproductions and precise descriptions. The international *Corpus vitrearum medii aevi*[52] was founded after the last war to take stock of all such glass, and to form a basis for the future history of the art as well as to encourage the study of methods of preservation.

In the last ten years or so a new technique for making pictures in coloured glass has developed, which no longer uses leads with inserted thin disks of glass, but produces the so-called beton-glass windows, composed of thick pieces of split glass, usually pot metal glass, held together by a mixture of cement. In fact, however, this technique is not really an innovation: known as the *claustra* technique, it was used in Mohammedan art. Moreover, one can hardly refer to most of the works of this style as glass-painting in the old sense of the word, because there is no painting with black manganese on the glass, nor does the cement form any real joints, but often consists of large masses, determining the motifs themselves; furthermore, many of the modern windows contain abstract designs.

The history of stained glass and its technique shows how much this art has been influenced by the spirit of each age. It followed the austerity of the Romanesque buildings, and then took over the new religious and mystical striving expressed in Gothic art, symbolising it by the light which poured through the stained glass windows into the cathedrals, and illuminated their dim interiors as the position of the sun and clouds permitted at any given moment.

Here light reveals itself in its unique form, its radiant translucency, while we see it only as a reflection on the surface of other paintings, or—in fact—of most natural objects. This light in the cathedrals, so impressive yet incalculable, seems not of this earth, and tends to produce a feeling of the presence of something transcendent, a feeling that many a modern man may share with those who in the Middle Ages first entered the Gothic churches.

DESCRIPTION OF PLATES

1. *Wissembourg (Alsace): Disk with Head of Christ*

This disk was found in the north of Alsace near Wissembourg in 1880. It came from the church of the Benedictine Abbey of SS. Peter and Paul, built between 1030 and 1070. For some time it was in private hands, but in 1923 it was acquired by the Frauenhaus Museum at Strasbourg.

It is probably the oldest known glass-painting in Europe, unless the fragments of the so-called roundel from Lorsch in Hesse, now in the Landesmuseum at Darmstadt, or the head in the crypt of the cathedral at Magdeburg, destroyed during the last war, can really be dated to the year 1000. An equally early date has also been considered for the Wissembourg disk, but one in the twelfth century is more probable.

The disk shows a frontal view of Christ's head with a blue-green and red medallion-like glass border; but the border may have been added in the nineteenth century. It is important to note that the grisaille painting in three distinct grades of intensity conforms to the rules given at the end of the eleventh century by Theophilus in his *Diversarium artium schedula*. The unevenness and the coarseness of the greenish disk are characteristic of this early date, though the very dark lines added to the face may have been touched up later on.

29

Another characteristic of the period is the use of black manganese to produce an ornamental effect, and to stress the flat mask-like appearance of the face with its large black eyes, giving the impression of a truly magical presence.

Parallels are to be found only in illuminated manuscripts and in gold and ivory works of the tenth and eleventh centuries.

2–3. *Augsburg Cathedral: The Prophets*

The figures of Jonah, Moses, David, Daniel, and Hosea, which originally belonged to a long series of figures of prophets, have survived in the clerestory windows of the cathedral at Augsburg. They are eight feet six inches high, standing upright, and although placed so high up they are most impressive. They show a certain amount of gesticulation, and the flesh parts stand out from the background in a manner quite foreign to that of the Wissembourg roundel; otherwise, however, the figures appear one-dimensional and are distributed ornamentally all over the window-panes like figures in a pack of cards.

The central vertical bands of the otherwise whitish backgrounds are coloured so as to show up the outlines of the beards and the hair. The garments, shoes, and hats are painted in strong colours with a predominance of green and red.

It seems likely that the figures were originally surrounded by a border, as they now appear somewhat tightly squeezed into the high windows, almost as if cut short at the edges; this is particularly noticeable in the picture of Jonah (plate 2a), where nearly eight inches have been cut off from the mouth of the whale, so that only a feeble indication of it remains.

A comparison suggests itself here with the miniatures of the Hirsau School, which also date from 1130–1140, though the stained glass of Augsburg is more impressive, not so much because of the size of the figures as because of the unknown artists' profound conception of the theme. As the stained glass of the Ottonian cathedrals has not survived, the Augsburg windows form one of the greatest art treasures of Germany.

4. *Poitiers Cathedral: The Crucifixion*

In the flat end of the chancel of St. Peter's cathedral of Poitiers, there is a central window of nearly twenty-seven feet in height, with beautiful medieval stained glass. Its main subject is a crucifixion, which as it were culminates in the round arch with a picture of the ascension of Christ. Louis Grodecki wrote of it in *Le vitrail français* (Paris, Edit. Deux Mondes, 1958), page 98: "The Crucifixion of Poitiers with the brilliance of its red, which spreads far into the light blue and soft green at the sides, forms the most beautiful piece of stained glass of the twelfth century; its magnificent effect can be compared only to that of the clerestory windows in the chancel of the cathedral at Chartres, dating from the thirteenth century."

The fine lines are still drawn in the elongated Romanesque style as in the Ascension of Christ at Le Mans. Overcome by suffering, Christ stands with His feet on a suppedaneum on the red cross, which is surrounded by an edging of blue palmettes, while Mary and John, and Longinus with the lance and the centurion with the sponge of vinegar, are to His right and left. In two pictures above the bar of the cross the disciples look sadly up to their master, hovering majestically in a mandorla, which is disappearing from their sight; the two angels carrying the mandorla are fitted with a superb mastery of rhythm into the spandrels to the right and left of it.

31

In the border at the bottom the Marys are to be seen at the grave; below this scene follow pictures of the resurrection of Christ and scenes from the lives of Peter and Paul; these are not shown in the reproduction.

Textual criticism by Crozet has disproved an earlier assumption that these windows were presented by Henry II and Elinore of Aquitaine, for their style suggests that they are contemporary with the building of the east chancel, which was completed between 1160 and 1180.

5. Reims, Saint Rémi: The Crucifixion

Standing to the south of the famous cathedral of Reims is the Benedictine Abbey of Saint Rémi (St. Remigius), interesting for the solemn architecture of its interior as well as for its precious stained glass. When the church was restored after the war, most of the early Gothic panes were replaced in very suitable modern frames by the glass-painter Simon of Reims. Thus the Crucifixion, dating from the time when the east chancel was finished in 1189/1190, took up once again the position it occupied before the bombardment of 1914; it shines down with its restrained brilliance from the central window of the apse at the height of the galleries.

The total height of the window is just under twelve feet. It has naturally suffered in the course of the centuries, so that several parts have had to be replaced, yet as a whole it is still a document of artistic and historical importance, dating from the end of the twelfth century.

Christ is shown patiently suffering; He is held by four nails to the cross, but there is no apparent heaviness or pathos, and as He does not hang from the cross, but stands (almost in a refined way) on a suppedaneum, a board below which there is a chalice to collect His blood and a skull as a sign that Christ conquers death and frees mankind of the everlasting death of sin. In place of the letters INRI the hand of God the Father is to be seen above Christ's head, blessing Him, while at either side of Him there are the slender figures of Mary and John, mourning Him. According to the nineteenth-century archaeologist Didron, the strange flowers put cross-wise into the space over their heads symbolise heliotropes.

A unique character is bestowed upon this picture by the lovely shading of its shining blue, its firm grisaille technique, the effect of which has been emphasised by abrading and wiping off, and by the network of leads, particularly well adapted to the design.

6–12. *Chartres: The Cathedral*

The cathedral of Notre Dame at Chartres represents the culmination of the medieval art of stained glass in France. There are no less than 173 windows with a total surface of over 21,500 square feet. We can only imagine the extent and the splendour of the stained glass of the early building, which was for the most part destroyed by fire in the year 1194. Some prominent items have survived, however, among others "The Tree of Jesse," "The Life of Christ," "The Passion," and a picture of the Virgin known as *Notre Dame de la Belle Verrière*. The narthex too, together with its windows, built between 1145 and 1155, was spared by the fire, and the reconstruction of the destroyed parts of the building was started soon after the catastrophe, so that according to the *Gesta Philippi Augusti* the high vaults were already completed by 1220 or 1221.

6–7. *Chartres: The Annunciation and The Visitation*

These two pictures are one above the other in the central window in the apse of the chancel, while in the pointed arch above them the Coronation of the Virgin, patroness of the church, is shown in a strictly frontal attitude like that of *Le Belle Verrière*. The stained glass of the chancel and its ambulatory dates from 1216–1230. The central window of the apse was very early on considered the most important of the high windows of the church, and a report on a restoration in 1415 spoke of it as the *Haute Verrière de Notre Dame*. Both this window and the next one to the north of it were presented by the bakers' guild, as one can see from the insignia reproduced in the lower part of the window.

In both pictures there are double arcades, their upper parts plain and linear; they separate and at the same time unite the Virgin and the angel of the Annunciation, and the Virgin and Elisabeth respectively. The monumental quality of this axial window is enhanced by the use of large scale figures, and as all four of them are treated in the same manner the balance of the composition as a whole is increased, while the majestic poise of the figures in no way reduces the individuality of their expressions and of their strongly emphasised gestures. All lines and colours within the contours are clearly stressed, and it is in particular the intensity of the colour with its basic tone of red and blue, and the rich edging of the window-frame by a broad ornamental band, which give a festive appearance to the pictures as a whole.

The Annunciation. The archangel Gabriel, conscious of his momentous mission, intimates the joyous news to Mary, over whose head the Holy Ghost hovers in the shape of a dove with a halo. Mary herself is clearly bewildered by the news. Canon Yves Delaporte has stated in his work on the stained glass at Chartres that he thinks he has found in this picture an analogy to a Syrian manuscript of the sixth century, which is in the National Library of Paris (B.N. Ms. syr. 33).

The Visitation. Contrasting with the picture of the Annunciation, the Virgin here looks much older, almost of the same age as Elisabeth, whom she seems about to embrace. The ceremonious rigidity of their attitudes increases the formal and static appearance of the pictures, which, however, are slightly relieved by the colourful contrast of the garments.

The window was restored by H. Gaudin in 1920.

8. *Chartres: The Good Samaritan*

The window, the middle part of which is reproduced here, was presented by the cobblers' guild between 1200 and 1215. The popular parable of the good Samaritan is depicted in an ornamental combination of quatrefoils, half quatrefoils, and round medallions, framed by white palmettes and fine spandrels filled with a chequered blue and red pattern.

At the bottom to the left, with the inscription *Samaritanus*, the good Samaritan assists the traveller. In the medallion next to it the traveller is helped on to his horse, and to the right the innkeeper waits for him in the doorway, and then cares for his charge in the lowest part of the quatrefoil above the medallion. The remainder of the disk is dedicated to the story of Adam and Eve: to the left the creation of Adam, in the centre Adam under the trees of Eden, to the right the creation of Eve, and on top, God the Father with Adam and Eve by the tree of knowledge. Above, though not shown in the reproduction, follow the fall of man, the expulsion from paradise, and the promise of the Saviour, who appears on top in the arch above the story of Cain and Abel.

The fleeting, well-nigh dancing movements of the slim figures suggest the same artists as in Bourges, though with some interval of time; nor can one deny a certain influence from the south-west of France, that is Le Mans and Poitiers, two modes of interpretation which need not be mutually exclusive.

35

9. *Chartres: The Window from the Guild of the Wine Merchants*

This window consists of medallions grouped in fours, each four partly covered by a fifth in the centre. The two centre medallions indicate that the window was donated by the wine merchants, as the lower, the more beautiful one, depicts a carter transporting a wine barrel, and in the medallion above—only partly visible in the reproduction—a barrel is being broached. The remaining six medallions reproduced here contain scenes from the life of St. Lubin or Leobin, Abbot of Brou and after 544 Bishop of Chartres, who died between 552 and 567. In the bottom medallion to the left the saint appears as a shepherd, because he came from peasant stock in the vicinity of Poitiers. To the right he is taught to read by a monk and above he studies busily while guarding his flock; then opposite this he is seen accompanied to the monastery by his father, and above this the abbot blesses him as he admits him to the monastic community.

10. *Chartres: Melchizedek, King David, and St. Anne*

These three windows together with two others, Solomon and Aaron, are in the north wall of the transept of the cathedral. Under a painted Gothic canopy of severe shape Melchizedek holds in his left hand chalice and bread, the symbols of the sacrifice of the New Covenant, while in his right hand he swings a censer. In the bottom part of some of these windows a figure contrasting to that above is shown in reduced size, here King Nebuchadnezzar kneeling before an idol.

In the next window King David, a magnificent old man, strikes a stately attitude as he plays the harp with ten strings (Psalm 32, 2). Below, King Saul stabs himself to death to escape the Philistines after his defeat near Gilboa (Kings, 31, 4).

In the third window there is St. Anne with Mary as a child in her arms. In her right hand she holds the tripartite lily; at her feet are the arms of France. St. Anne was greatly revered at Chartres, because at the beginning of the thirteenth century Count Louis had obtained the head of the saint at Constantinople, which his wife Catherine subsequently bequeathed to the cathedral.

The five figures of these windows were not chosen in a haphazard way: St. Anne, the central figure, distinguished from the others by its size, stands in an axial relation to the Virgin's window under the great rose. The Kings David and Solomon point to the kingdom of Christ, while Melchizedek and Aaron with the bishop's cope and the blooming rod point to the priesthood of Christ. The figures are full of movement, and their features striking, owing to the harsh gradation of the colours.

These windows were restored in 1886 by H. Bonnot.

11. *Chartres: The Life of Jesus*

The central window in the west façade is one of the largest and most beautiful in the cathedral: in twenty-seven disks the life of Christ is represented from the Annunciation to the entry into Jerusalem; the window culminates in the pointed arch with a picture of the Virgin and Child. The twelve lower disks are reproduced here; they are composed of three bands, medallions and square disks alternating, surrounded by fine edgings of palmettes and fabulous animals. The disks are arranged in the usual order, with the story reading from left to right and upwards. In the bottom tier therefore are shown the Annunciation, the Visitation, and the Nativity—the latter, as in medieval manuscript illuminations, with a profusion of detail; at the sides two curtains are drawn back to open the view into the room, in the centre of which the Christ Child lies in a crib raised on two arcades; the Virgin, who is resting, points with her right hand to her Child, while St. Joseph has fallen alseep at the foot of her bed. In the centre there is a lamp to light up the room, and the star appears at the side of the picture. In the next tier, in a lively scene, angels announce the birth of Christ to the shepherds. Next to them sit in a double arcade two scribes, searching in the Bible for the time of Christ's birth; with them is King Herod, who welcomes the three wise men as they arrive from the right. In the tier above they are on their way to the Virgin and the Child, to pay homage to Him with their gifts. Then we see them returning with empty hands, but still accompanied by the star. The sequence of the pictures is reversed in the next tier: to the right the wise men are roused by an angel and told to return home by a different route; then follow to the left the presentation in the temple and a medallion with three figures holding offerings.

12. *Chartres: Notre Dame de la Belle Verrière*

This beautiful and impressive window at the right-hand side of the chancel-ambulatory, which dates from about 1150, survived the fire of 1194. It was already known as *Notre Dame de la Belle Verrière* in the fifteenth century, a name emphasising the charm which emanates from this light figure in luminous blue on a bright red background, a charm which may have been partly responsible for the particular veneration in which this picture was held. This may also have been why Canon Geoffrey des Fausheiz was given permission in 1324 to erect an altar under this brilliant image. The figure of the Virgin covers three disks at a height of just over seven feet; she is shown seated on a throne, wearing a rich crown. The solemn Christ Child on her lap looks fixedly and searchingly at the observer, lifting His right hand to administer the blessing, and holding in His left hand a book on which the words from Isaiah, 40, 3–4, can be read: O(MN)IS/VA/LLI/S/I(M)PL/EB/IT/VR, "every valley shall be exalted."

13–23. *Bourges: The Cathedral*

All the disks reproduced here are from the chancel-ambulatory and the chapels in the chancel of the Cathedral of Saint Etienne. Between 1200 and 1209 under Bishop Guillaume the designs for the new cathedral were sanctioned and the work started. The chancel was probably finished by 1220, as the body of the bishop, who had in the meantime died and been canonised, was given a solemn burial behind the main altar on 7th May 1218. The nave was not completed until 1270 when St. Louis died.

In the high north windows of the chancel the prophets are represented in a solemn row, and opposite them in the south windows stand the apostles, both as if forming a retinue for the Saviour, who is to be seen in the centre. Themes from the history of the saints and the lives of local saints are depicted in the twenty-five windows of the ambulatory and the chapels.

In his searching study of the windows of Bourges, Georges Quiévreux established that two masters had worked there, dividing the work between them; both had probably also been employed in Chartres before 1215. As their names are unknown, Quiévreux called them Master A and Master B. The latter seems to have been the more important artist, as the Apocalypse window is attributed to him. He usually emphasised the folds of the garments and the features of the faces, for example by making a characteristic V-shaped wrinkle at the bridge of the nose, and it often seems as if the skeletons of his lean figures were showing through their tight garments. Beautiful stylised flower ornaments frequently frame the individual scenes in the quatrefoils, suggesting an affinity with the *Liber Floridus* of the twelfth century, which is in the National Library of Paris (B.N. Ms. lat. 8865).

Master A had a better knowledge of anatomy, his style as a whole was softer, and his lines are much smoother and thinner. It is difficult to say which of the two masters was the older.

13. *Bourges: The Christ of the Apocalypse*

The third, very impressive window to the south in the chancel-ambulatory of the cathedral, ascribed to Master B, is dedicated to the Apocalypse (Quiévreux XX). In three quatrefoils, one above the other, this eschatological theme is combined with those of the foundation of the church, the true presence of Christ (here reproduced) and the glory of the everlasting church.

In the picture below that reproduced here Christ stands as judge of the world, the sword in His mouth, seven stars hanging from His outstretched hand, stars above His head, and seven candlesticks at His side. In the top quatrefoil Christ appears with the standard of the cross and the Book, accompanied by two angels. In the middle quatrefoil, reproduced here, Christ is seen enthroned, distributing the Holy Spirit in the shape of fiery tongues. In accordance with the theme the colouring is solemn, the deep blue being relieved by glowing red.

14. *Bourges: The Angel of the Last Judgment*

This picture is a detail of the window reproduced on plate 21. The angel, beautifully fitted into the upper curve of a half quatrefoil open towards the outside edge of the picture, stands tall and slim with light coloured wings, a green tunic, and a purple cloak, on a bank of clouds decorated with festoons, such as was frequently used from the early twelfth century to the late Middle Ages to indicate celestial regions. Blowing his long trumpet he announces the Last Judgment, and under the bank of clouds (not to be seen in the reproduction) the dead leave their graves. The rather sombre colouring and the way the lines are drawn indicate the work of Master A.

15. Bourges: Christ from St. Mary Magdalene's Window

The window in the first chapel of the apse to the left is a companion to the window of St. Mary of Egypt. In the section reproduced here Christ appears immediately after the resurrection, with the open grave in the background to the right. With the words *Noli me tangere* He turns away from Mary Magdalene, who had sadly enquired after him (John, 20, 14). Christ, having conquered death, has lost all earthly heaviness and walks, half hovering, almost dancing, with very lively gestures and a lively expression on His face. The severe treatment of the garments, the slenderness of the limbs, and the strongly contrasting colours suggest the hand of Master B.

16–19. Bourges: Window of St. Mary of Egypt

These four panels belong to the first window in the north chapel of the cloisters, and illustrate (in accordance with the *Legenda aurea*) events from the life of the saint. As the majority of these panels contain only one figure each, it is somewhat difficult to understand the sequence of the pictures, which are shown in tiers of three panels each, for example plates 16, 17, and 19.

On plate 16 Mary leaves the house, on plate 19 a young man meets her, soliciting her with a gesture of his hand, while in the disk in the centre (plate 17) Mary holds a pilgrim's staff, and the priest shows her the way to church. The disks are painted in rich colours; the charm of most of them is intensified by flowers and trees added to the pictures.

Although neither this kind of composition nor any similar arrangement of individual disks is to be found anywhere outside this chapel, it is assumed generally that the author was Master B.

20. *Bourges: The Story of Joseph*

The first window on the south side of the chancel-ambulatory, dedicated to the story of Joseph, is composed of several large disks, each ending in four leaves with pointed curves, joined by small medallions to other disks.

In the disk at the bottom, part of it cut away by the edge of the picture, Joseph is seen dreaming about the seven sheaves of his brothers making obeisance to his own sheaf, and there is also a hint of his second dream "the sun and the moon and the eleven stars made obeisance to me" (Gen. 37, 9).

In the disk with the pointed curve there is Jacob sending Joseph with a basket of bread to seek his brothers, who in the medallion above this one keep watch for him so that they may speedily realise their vile scheme. This theme was also treated in a window in the cathedral at Chartres in a similar composition and like style, so that it seems clear that the window at Bourges was made by Master A, who had probably worked at Chartres until 1215.

21. *Bourges: The Last Judgment*

The first window to the right of the chapel in the apse of the chancel-ambulatory is compiled of quatrefoils placed squarely, each ending in four leaves with pointed curves, and of half quatrefoils open outwards. Scenes of the Last Judgment are depicted on it, for instance in the detail reproduced here the separation of the righteous from the wicked. To the left an angel offers to lead the chosen to paradise—on the panel still further to the left (and not reproduced here) Abraham receives them to his bosom—while to the right the devil with blue body and red head takes the damned—who include both ecclesiastical and secular dignitaries—to hell, whose mouth swallows them up still further to the right; but this is not reproduced here. In the upper part of this plate the archangel Michael, holding the scales in his left hand, saves some souls from the fiend.

This window, in itself dark, also suffers from a thick incrustation on the outside so that the outlines of many of the figures can only be seen with difficulty. It is an impressive and lively work of art, and the restrained colouring suggests that it should be ascribed to Master B.

22. *Bourges: The Parable of Dives and Lazarus*

The first window to the north in the chancel-ambulatory contains impressive pictures of incidents from St. Luke's Gospel. Medallions and quatrefoils alternate

on a shining blue background, always three in a row. In the medallion reproduced here the rich man is shown as he sits clad in a red robe and with a green
cloak lined with ermine, while a servant pours out wine for him. This illustrates
Luke, 12, 19–20: "I will say to my soul: Soul thou hast much goods laid up for
many years; take thine ease, eat, drink, and be merry. But God said unto him:
Thou fool, this night thy soul shall be required of thee." In the disks above this
one there are the feast of the rich man, the death of Lazarus, his reception into
heaven, and the rejection of the rich man—a theme which became very popular
towards the end of the Middle Ages through the *Ars moriendi*.

In the quatrefoil below the medallion, masons, whose guild had donated the
window, are shown at work.

The gay colouring and the drapery of the garments make it probable that
Master A was the artist of this window.

23. *Bourges: The Deliverance of St. Peter*

The middle window in the second chapel to the left in the apse is dedicated
to the lives of St. Peter and St. Paul, the chief of the apostles. The quarter of the
medallion reproduced here represents the deliverance of St. Peter by an angel.
By virtue of its colouring and composition the picture is vivid and effective.
Master A, presumably its author, has shown great skill in depicting Peter,
suddenly wakened from his sleep and listening half amazed and half hesitant to
the instructions of the angel; he is already free of his fetters, holding in his hands
the stone to which they were fastened.

A vertical band at the edges, and a background filled with red squares with
larger light blue quatrefoils and smaller white ones at their points of intersection,
fill the corner and form part of the frame of the medallion.

24. *Meissen Cathedral: Holy Mass*

In the apse of the cathedral at Meissen in Saxony there is a symbolic window of great interest. As part of the genealogy of Christ the kings of Israel are shown in the central band of the picture, which is crowned by a mandorla with Christ the Teacher. To the left is a series of pictures from the Old Testament, opposite them scenes from the New Testament referring to them. Holy Mass is represented simply but impressively at the moment of the elevation of the Host. The altar at which it is celebrated appears to have been rotated by ninety degrees, in defiance of perspective, in order to enable the viewer to see both priest and altar from the best possible angle. As the cathedral had been destroyed by fire in 1207, and the reconstruction was begun towards 1220, the panel may be dated as from the middle of the thirteenth century.

25. *Mönchen-Gladbach, The Abbey Church: Virgin and Child*

The fine symbolic central window in the apse of the former Benedictine Abbey of St. Veit (St. Vitus) has been preserved. Its left half consists of a series of eight-leaved medallions on a geometrical background design. Scenes from the Old Testament are depicted there, set opposite the right-hand half of the window, where scenes from the New Testament are held by intertwined scrolls of leaves, representing the tree of Jesse. In the third of these medallions is a picture, in subdued colours, of the adoration of the magi, a detail of which is the Virgin and Child reproduced here. The Virgin sits on a throne, the Child who administers the blessing sits on her lap; she seems surprised at the worship accorded to her divine Son.

As pendant to this picture the queen of Sheba visiting Solomon is shown in the left-hand series.

The new chancel of the abbey founded in 759 was built in the second half of the thirteenth century by Gerhard, a master-builder from Cologne, and consecrated in 1275. It may therefore be assumed that the stained glass of the chancel dates from the seventh decade of the thirteenth century, especially as its style seems to confirm this. This so-called jagged style is even more pronounced in this picture than in the panels from the Dominican church now in the cathedral of Cologne; it was popular in Westphalia and Saxony, and also spread to the upper Rhine.

26. *Freiburg. Augustinian Museum: Christ Enthroned*

The museum of the Augustinians at Freiburg im Breisgau contains a beautiful six-leaved disk with the figure of Christ enthroned (Inv. No. 90/M), which probably came from the chancel of the late Romanesque minster. Though not striving for effect, the figure of Christ with its grey and white tunic and a blue cloak, against a fiery red background, appears both majestic and holy. Placed between an alpha and an omega, the right hand raised to give the blessing, the left holding the book, the figure as well as the throne with its high cushions are still Romanesque, while the drapery of the garment and the painting added to the figure already show a feeling for Gothic forms. One can thus fix the date of the disk at approximately 1240, when the reconstruction of the nave of the minster of Strasbourg was begun, where the first windows of the north triforium (with the figures of Christ's ancestors) show some affinity with this stained glass at Freiburg, although the art of Strasbourg of the first half of the thirteenth century seems heavier. It may therefore be said that there was a particular old Freiburg style in stained glass as well as in sculpture—a pleasing style, avoiding any harshness or heaviness, though this sometimes proved a disadvantage.

27. *St. Florian, Augustinian Monastery: Virgin and Child*

The Augustinian prebendal monastery of St. Florian in Upper Austria was reconstructed in the seventeenth century by Carlo Antonio Carlone, but part of the nave of the church, the crypt, and the south tower (which dated from the thirteenth century) were preserved.

A precious relic from that earlier epoch is the disk reproduced here. It is a work by Master Wolfhart, and though it dates from the end of the thirteenth century, the ornaments of the medallion (the yellow edging, the string of white pearls as well as the throne) still show something of a Romanesque appearance, and only the drapery of the garment, the refined lines, the blue background of naturalistic vine tendrils, and the colour contrasts point to the Gothic period. In fact the type of the Virgin with the Child standing on her lap and caressing her did not cross the Alps before the second half of the thirteenth century.

There is some affinity between this disk and a tracery rose window at Strasbourg, and some disks in the cloisters of the monastery at Wettingen in Switzerland.

28. *Cologne Cathedral: The Head of the Apostle Simon*

In the chapel of the chancel of St. Stephen in the cathedral at Cologne there is some stained glass with more than life-size figures of a row of apostles, which once belonged to the former Dominican church. The figures stand below painted trefoil arcades with pinnacles, as was usual at the period from which they date— about 1320. The background of the pictures is red, framed by a blue border with yellow knots. In the disk reproduced here we see the head of St. Simon, the only detail preserved from the original figure. Only the impressive head with the beautiful curly golden hair is old; beard, garment, and all the rest are new. The lively features of the face are a traditional characteristic of Simon Zelotes, who looks vigorously wide awake.

29. *Cologne Cathedral: A King from the Old Testament*

In the windows of the clerestory in the chancel of the cathedral there are the standing figures of forty-eight kings from the Old Testament. They measure about seven and a half feet in height, and hold sceptres and golden orbs in their hands; they stand in dignified attitudes on either side of the Virgin and Child in the window of the apse, forming their solemn retinue. Each of them stands under a painted canopy with pinnacles, against a background of which the colour alternates between red and blue. At their feet are the arms of the donors, the Counts of Holland, of Cleves, of Juliers, and those of the city of Cologne or noble families of Cologne.

Series of windows of this kind are often found in French cathedrals—for example in Chartres and Amiens, which at that time exercised considerable influence on the art of the Rhineland.

The detail reproduced here is taken from the window given by the Hardevust family of Cologne. It combines in its simple drawing a dignity of attitude with the wisdom and mildness of old age.

The windows were made between 1317 and 1320, certainly before the consecration of the chancel on 27th September 1322.

30. *Cologne Cathedral: John the Baptist*

This plate contains a detail from the window of the three wise men in St. Mary's Chapel in the chancel-ambulatory of the cathedral. To the left, above the main scene of the Adoration, John the Baptist stands under a pretty painted canopy, clad in a cloak of raw hides and pointing to the Lamb. The colours are restrained, but the portrait most expressive.

This panel is the best-preserved part of the window, which dates from the first quarter of the fourteenth century; in 1850 and again in 1900 it underwent some inexpert restorations.

31. *Heiligkreuztal (Swabia), Cistercian Abbey: Virgin and Child*

The church of the abbey of the Cistercian nuns at Heiligkreuztal was reconstructed between 1300 and 1350. During part of that time Elizabeth von Stepheln was abbess (1305–1312), and she is represented as the donor on her knees at the feet of the Virgin (not shown in the section reproduced here). It is highly probable that the superb series of forty panels, which fill the four bands of the east window in the chancel, were presented by her or at least begun in her lifetime.

Four main figures, all of the same height and similar colouring, fill the lower two tiers of the window. They are the Virgin (reproduced here), St. Verena of Zurzach, worshipped in particular in the vicinity of the Bodensee, St. Catherine, and St. Agnes. They are painted in the so-called soft style of 1300, "a special variety of maidenly sentimentality and decorative beauty of lines," as H. Wentzel described it. They stand in frontal attitudes, their bodies somewhat inclined, their heads in half profile, slightly bowed. The Virgin on the panel reproduced here turns pensively to the Christ Child, who rests on her left arm and plays with an apple. The haloes serve the practical purpose of giving better colour contrast, and thus a three-dimensional effect, as so often in stained glass.

This window is no doubt one of the finest examples of the stained glass associated with Konstanz.

32. *Munich, Liebfrauenkirche: St. Margaret with the Dragon*

St. Margaret of Antioch was won over to Christianity by her wet-nurse, and suffered martyrdom under Diocletian. The palm in her left hand is the symbol of martyrdom, the dragon in her right hand her emblem. According to the thirteenth-century account in the Golden Legend, she asked God during her imprisonment to show her the fiend, whereupon a dragon came into her prison and tried to attack and devour her, but vanished again as soon as she made the sign of the cross. St. Margaret is one of the fourteen helpers in need, popular in the West since the twelfth century; she is mainly worshipped as a helper in cases of difficult child-birth.

The window reproduced here is in the vestry of the Liebfrauenkirche (Church of Our Lady) at Munich. All the details of style, especially the dignified and refined attitude of the figure, the broad folds of the garment with its soft lines, the thin lattice with quatrefoils in the background, and not least the naturalistic representation of the oak leaves on the border painted in grisaille on a red foundation, points to a date later than 1320.

33. *Strasbourg, Frauenhaus Museum: St. John the Evangelist*

This refined, somewhat stylised figure of St. John the Evangelist forms part of the large window in the apse of the former parish church at Mutzig in Alsace. After the church had been demolished in 1879 to be replaced by a neo-Gothic one, the Society for the Preservation of the Historical Monuments in Alsace acquired the stained glass, which is now in the Frauenhaus Museum at Strasbourg.

The window, which is in an excellent state of preservation, measures over thirteen feet in height, and consists of twelve panels with architecture painted in grisaille, and with small figures. Between two rather fine columns with yellow head-pieces, fitted into masonry which is painted a light colour, stands the slim figure of Christ's beloved disciple, painted with brilliant colours and strong lines and standing out well against the blue pattern of the background.

This pattern—small crosses formed of leaves—also occurs in the Königsfelden series of windows twenty years later. (See plates 36, 38–41.)

34, 35. *Herford, Johanneskirche: The Nativity and the Flight into Egypt*

Several beautiful panels of the fourteenth century have survived in the Johanneskirche (St. John's Church) at Herford in Westphalia. Owing to their strong colours, their luminosity has not suffered much from the impact of the weather. Of particular interest is the fact that the small white flowers in the Virgin's cloak were abraded quite early on by the use of a flashed glass technique.

Each of the two pictures reproduced here is fitted into a quatrefoil with the corners left empty, and these quatrefoils are set into a central band resembling a red carpet. The arrangement of the figures follows the tradition of the *Biblia pauperum* of the thirteenth century.

The Christ Child turning towards his Mother in the Nativity scene, and the youthful appearance of Joseph, who in the picture of the Flight into Egypt seems full of solicitude for Mary, are particularly striking.

36, 38–41. *Königsfelden, in Switzerland*

The church at Königsfelden was erected to serve a double convent for Franciscans and Clares founded by Elisabeth, the widow of the German King Albrecht I, on the spot where he was murdered by his nephew on 1st May 1308. The building of the church, which possesses perhaps the finest stained glass in the whole of Switzerland, was begun in 1310, though the consecration of the chancel had to be postponed until 1330. All the windows were donated by sons of Albrecht, and date from 1318 to 1335. The chancel alone contains eleven high windows, of which five panels are reproduced here.

They are in a particularly charming style, evolved by the workshop of the Habsburg court—an art of which the influence was felt in Alsace and as far as Swabia. But the first suggestion for the painted architecture in these windows probably came from Strasbourg, because what stained glass remains there from St. Thomas's Church, as well as the panel in the Frauenhaus Museum (plate 33), shows the same features. About 1330, however, the roles were reversed and the art of the court of the Habsburgs, as represented at Königsfelden, became responsible for the style of the windows in the south transept of the minster at Strasbourg.

36. *Königsfelden: Brother Leo reads the Gospels*

The eighth window in the north façade is entirely dedicated to the story of

St. Francis of Assisi. In the detail reproduced here Brother Leo sits at the foot of a rock; he opens the Gospels three times to enquire into the will of God, and each time comes upon the beginning of the story of the Passion; the spirit of the *Fioretti* of St. Francis or of Bonaventura or Thomas of Celano is apparent here.

The simple figure of Brother Leo stands out well from the red-patterned background of the medallion; its blue spandrels are decorated with the Habsburg lions, of which one is partly visible in the reproduction. At the bottom of the window is the portrait of the donor, Duke Otto of Habsburg.

37. *Strasbourg, Frauenhaus Museum: The Archangel Gabriel*

This lovely panel is in the Frauenhaus Museum at Strasbourg. Though the red and blue background framed by a row of white pearls is a nineteenth-century addition, it is nevertheless quite harmonious and fits in with the style of the first half of the fourteenth century, from which epoch the panel dates. The plain clear drawing is reminiscent of the panel from Mutzig (plate 33), but the treatment of the features and of the hair is more subtle. The combination of wings with the half-kneeling pose relieves the figure of any terrestrial heaviness, and gives it a delicate rhythm, which is enhanced by the gesture of the arms and by the flying banderol. Perfect harmony is established in this picture through the exquisite use of colour.

38. *Königsfelden: The Adoration of the Magi*

The scene of the Adoration covers all three panels of one tier. To the left—

not reproduced here—stands Caspar, in the centre panel are Melchior and Balthasar, and to the right the Virgin and Child. The young King Melchior stands pointing to the star, which appears in the trefoil above the right-hand panel, but cannot be seen in the reproduction. This conforms to the traditional arrangement of the scene, popular in many medieval paintings. King Balthasar has reverently removed his crown to do homage to the Christ Child. The delicate nuances of the colours are a suitable choice for the noble and rather lively attitudes of the kings.

39. *Königsfelden: Virgin and Child*

This panel is the continuation to the right of the Adoration scene. The Christ Child turns towards the wise men with a lively awareness; the gesture of His hands in particular is remarkable. The Virgin supports Him gently with her right hand, holding in her left a rose, the symbol of love and of the sacrifice she will make when she gives up her Son. The artist has depicted her pensive attitude with very great skill. The colours are adapted to those of the picture as a whole, even with regard to the quatrefoil motif in the blue squares of the pattern in the background. This window was presented by Duke Leopold of Austria and his wife Catherine of Savoy, who died in 1326, so that it must have been put in before that year.

40. *Königsfelden: St. Christopher*

This panel and the next form part of St. Anne's window. The cult of St.

Christopher can be traced back in the East to the fifth century, and his representation as we know it (and as it appears here) follow the account in the *Legenda aurea* of Jacobus de Voragine in 1288. The popular belief *Christophori faciem die quacumque tueris ille nempe die morte mala non morieris* ("On whatever day you see the face of Christopher you will not die a bad death") has contributed considerably to his popularity. As the most efficacious of the fourteen helpers in need, his figure was put close to the doors or against pillars in medieval cathedrals, and appears frequently both as a fresco on the walls and in the stained glass of the windows.

Against a background of blue bull's-eye panes with abraded small rosettes the figure of the saint stands out in brilliant colours, though it is also a little stiff and expressionless; the Christ Child sits on the saint's left shoulder with an expression of supreme confidence.

Perhaps this window too was presented—as was its pendant—by Duke Leopold of Austria and Catherine of Savoy, but there can be no absolute certainty of this.

41. *Königsfelden: An Angel*

This is not the archangel Gabriel announcing the Incarnation to the Virgin, but the angel announcing to St. Anne the birth of her daughter Mary, as described in the apocryphal gospel of the pseudo-Matthew. The banderol held by the angel, who stands in a statuesque attitude, refers to this: *QVONIA | I | CONSILIO | DEI | ES | GERM | TVV* (*Quoniam in consilio Dei est germen tuum*); the inscription has been restored.

In the same window there is also a picture of the annunciation to Joachim.

55

42. Mulhouse, Stephanskirche: The Flight into Egypt

In the Church of St. Stephen, which was demolished in 1858 and replaced by a neo-Gothic building in 1866, is preserved one of the largest and most interesting symbolic sequences of stained glass of the whole fourteenth century; it dates from 1330. Each scene is represented in a group of three panels, the picture from the New Testament always lying in the middle. The Flight into Egypt reproduced here is placed (according to the *Speculum humanae salvationis* of the fourteenth century) between an Egyptian idol, showing a maiden with a child, and that of young Moses before Pharaoh. Resigned to the will of God, a remarkably elderly Joseph walks confidently at the command of the angel so as to save Mother and Child from persecution by Herod. The tree in the background and the fine ornament in the keel-arch form a harmonious apex for the well-composed group. The scale of glowing colours used here is strong yet restrained, with the lighter parts greatly enhancing the three-dimensional effect.

43–45. Viktring, Cistercian Abbey

The windows in the chancel of the former Cistercian church at Viktring in Carinthia contain a sequence of sixty panels from the late fourteenth century, unique not only because the series is complete, but also because of the excellent state of preservation of most of it. Unfortunately, many of these windows are hidden behind a high, heavy altar-piece. Although this Cistercian monastery maintained close relations with its mother-house at Bettnach-Weiler near Metz, the stained glass was not commissioned in France. The style of the windows is strongly reminiscent of the art of the court at Vienna, and since the work on this subject by Kieslinger it is generally held that they came from the ducal workshop at Vienna. The highly developed style of this workshop spread from the cathedral and the church of Maria am Gestade (St. Mary on the Shore) in Vienna to the chapel at Ebreichsdorf, to St. Erhard in Styria (plate 48), and as far as Viktring in Carinthia.

Particularly attractive is the treatment of the background in the panels of this window, of which M. Frodl stated: "The background resembles a moving sea of scrolls of flat leaves, from which the covering colour has been carefully abraded, making the rich red, blue, or green of the glass shine in the changing light like the facets of precious stones."

Judging by the figures of the donors, the windows were not made before 1378, and probably about 1390.

43. *Viktring, Cistercian Abbey: The Ascension of Christ*

The main theme of the pictures in the central window of the apse is the story of the Passion of Christ, ending with the Resurrection and the Ascension. The strict symmetry of the representation of the Ascension, traditional since the *Biblia pauperum*, is considerably relieved in the picture at Viktring by the contrasting brilliance of the colours. The apostles with the Virgin in the foreground are seen kneeling deeply moved in a half circle around a green hill, where there is still the imprint of the feet of Our Lord who has vanished above. Sometimes Christ Himself was not shown, but was indicated only by the imprint of His feet, though sometimes His feet and the seam of His cloak were also shown. This manner of representation has a parallel in Buddhist art, as Buddha also left his footprints behind on the spot where he had been meditating, as he departed from the material world.

44. *Viktring, Cistercian Abbey: The Annunciation*

This detail from one of the north windows of the apse presents the Virgin making a gesture of amazement as she receives the angel's message. The fine panel is made very impressive through its sincerity of feeling, its vivid charm, the competent linear drawing of the drapery, and the brilliant and rich colouring. Both figures—only one of Gabriel's hands is visible on the reproduction—stand out vividly against the dark blue festoons in the background. Unfortunately the impact made on this window by the weather through the centuries is clearly noticeable at several points.

45. *Viktring, Cistercian Abbey: Christ bearing the Cross*

Among the scenes of the Passion in the central window of the apse, that of Christ bearing the Cross is the most animated, although this does not show in the small detail reproduced here. In obedience to the will of God the Father, Christ has taken up the Cross and drags Himself laboriously along under the attacks of His tormentors. The yellow Cross contrasts vividly with the bluish purple of Christ's garment. By thin brush-strokes and delicate shaping, as well as by abrading regular strips of the coloured background in the section of the picture showing the hair, the artist has portrayed the Passion with deep feeling, but without any superficial sentimentality.

46–47. *Munich, Frauenkirche: The Visitation*

This Bavarian picture of the Visitation, simple though deeply compassionate in feeling, dates from 1425; it is in the Maffei Kapelle of the Liebfrauenkirche (Church of Our Lady) at Munich. There are two panels forming a unit, and showing under a double arcade the meeting of Elisabeth with the Virgin; both are serenely and happily anticipating their miraculous motherhood. The representation of the offspring in their wombs is in keeping with the naïve and reverent outlook of the Middle Ages. The unborn John the Baptist is shown on his knees worshipping little Jesus who wears a halo, so adding an innocent and playful touch to the picture. The figures of the mothers contrast with each other; the soft violet of Elisabeth's garment—she looks considerably older than the Virgin— probably symbolises repentance and the advent, and points to the preaching of John, the forerunner of Jesus. The Virgin wears a cloak of pale blue and glowing red over a whitish garment.

48. *St. Erhard in Styria, Parish Church: The Virgin and Child*

In this parish church in Styria there is an interesting and well-preserved sequence of stained glass pictures with scenes from the life of Christ, presented by Duke Albrecht III, who died in 1395. At that time the so-called ducal workshop at Vienna exercised considerable influence upon the art of stained glass in parts of southern Austria, Styria, and Carinthia—for example upon that of the Cistercian abbey at Viktring.

The detail shown here is part of a Nativity scene; the Virgin is represented sitting, covering the Christ Child with the folds of her cloak in token of the close relationship between Mother and Child. There is a bed of straw beside her in the background. The artist has shown great mastery in the treatment of the deep folds of the garment, through striking yet delicate drawing and the effective simplicity of his colour scheme.

49. *Munich, Frauenkirche: The Christ Child from the Scharfzandt Window*

The central window at the end of the chancel in the Liebfrauenkirche (Church of Our Lady) was presented by the town councillor Wilhelm Scharfzandt, and made between 1482 and 1488 by Peter Hemmel von Andlau, the greatest glass-painter of the late Gothic era. Each scene in this window is crowned by a painted canopy formed of boughs, similar to those in the window known as the Kramer window (1478–80) in the minster at Ulm, and to the Volkamer window in St. Lorenz at Nuremberg (1486–87).

The detail reproduced here is the central part of a Nativity scene; with its magnificent colours and the technical mastery revealed in every detail, it bears eloquent witness to the skill and competence of its painter.

50. *Munich, Frauenkirche: The Annunciation*

The series of fifty-eight panels, to which this Annunciation belongs, represents scenes from the *Speculum humanae salvationis* of the fourteenth century. As the name of the artist who made this window in 1480 is unknown, it is usually referred to as the *"speculum* window." The customary schematic representation is here given a new charm through details suggested by the general style of the epoch, and by the painter's technical ability. Almost every technique of the art of stained glass is used: grisaille, silvery yellow, the abrading of parts of the coloured layer of glass, and the lightening of the pearls in the border of the angel's cloak by the cutting-out technique. The scene is framed by a finely painted Renaissance arcade of branches.

51. Munich, Frauenkirche: The Angel at the Pool at Bethesda

The angel who troubled the water in the pool at Bethesda, which healed those stepping into it (John, 5, 2–4), is depicted here inside a richly decorated arcade with a wide landscape in the background; he is portrayed bending down to stir the water with both his hands.

This scene had already been used early on in Christian iconography—for instance in the frescoes of the third century in the chapel at Dura Europos in Syria, and in the catacombs of St. Peter and Marcellinus in Rome in the fourth century (compare O. Frankl, *Der Meister des Speculum Fensters von 1480 in der Münchner Frauenkirche*, Berlin, 1932).

In accordance with the *Speculum humanae salvationis*, Moses, smiting the rock to draw water from it, is shown as the Old Testament pendant to this angel.

52. Munich, Frauenkirche: The Feast from the Window of the Wine Merchants' Guild

This is a panel from the former Salvator Church, which was erected in 1494 by Duke Albrecht IV as church for the cemetery. The glass-painters came from the workshop of the Liebfrauenkirche. The stained glass dates from the end of the fifteenth century, and is similar in style to that of the Liebfrauenkirche. Next to the panel of the wine merchants is that of the butchers, dated 1499.

The rich gold and silver vessels might almost suggest that the window was presented by the guild of the goldsmiths, rather than by the wine merchants, but the cheerful atmosphere of a wine shop is very well depicted; the old man in the foreground seems to be giving serious consideration to something his neighbour has said to him, while the man to the right seems extremely pleased with the banquet; all these men are typical representatives of the dignified and self-confident burghers of the late Middle Ages.

The drawing in the panel is so powerful as to be reminiscent of a woodcut. All the lighter parts are done in grisaille, and juxtaposed to them are rich colours, contrasting strongly with each other—a characteristic feature of this epoch of so many contrasts.

53. *Chaumont en Vexin, Parish Church: The Birth of John the Baptist (c. 1547)*

This tripartite composition in the parish church at Chaumont en Vexin, near Gisors in Normandy, accurately depicts the interior of a Renaissance burgher's home. There is a room with a ceiling of heavy beams; a high window to the left gives access to the daylight, and through an open door in the background a landscape is visible. Elisabeth's bed stands in the centre of the room; its high head-board is shaped like a volute and ends in the head of a faun. On the mantlepiece in the left-hand corner there are some very fine slender jugs. Dumb Zacharias sits in priestly robes in the left foreground, writing on a board: "His name is John" (Luke, 1, 63). Servants are busy bathing the new-born Child.

The colouring is very different from that used in the Middle Ages; sepia-grisaille and a translucent violet contrast sharply with brilliant, cold colours such as green and blue. But this heavy and saturated colouring is relieved by a golden yellow and by grisaille; the influence of the School of Fontainebleau, with its admixture of Bolognese art, is obvious.

A nearby window showing the decapitation of John the Baptist is dated 1547, and though it is evidently the work of a different artist, the same date probably applies to the whole series of stained glass in the church.

62

54. *Private Collection, Nalini Jayasuriya, Ceylon: A Singhalese Annunciation*

Nalini Jayasuriya has represented in this stained glass, in the style of her own country, a theme which is traditionally Christian in its representation. Although stained glass as a form of art is not known in the culture of her part of the world, she has created some remarkably successful work with her versatile talent, her intuition, and her inherent feeling of form. She was born in 1926 in Ceylon of Protestant parents and Buddhist ancestors, and later became a Catholic. She is extremely versatile, and works not only in stained glass, but also makes pottery, terracotta, paints on silk, and works in yet other media. The Annunciation reproduced here was made in the workshop of the *Hofkunstanstalt und Glasmalerei* of Franz Mayer at Munich; it was exhibited during the Eucharistic World Congress in Munich in 1960.

Both the figures in the picture stand out against the dark background like silhouettes in an Indian or Javanese shadow-play. Their grace is reminiscent of Indian miniatures, and their swaying, subtle poses suggest fashionable *bayadères* (Hindu temple dancing-girls). The drawing of the mouths and eyes is typical of the art of the East. The lines of the drawing undulate like lianas, and this exotic element in the ornamentation shows a certain affinity with the *Jugendstil* which was common in Munich about 1920. The heavenly messenger carries a lotus blossom in place of the traditional lily.

55. *Private Collections, Hans Gottfried von Stockhausen: Easter Morning*

"And when the sabbath was past, Mary Magdalene, and Mary the mother of James, and Salome, bought spices, so that they might go and anoint Him. And very early on the first day of the week, they went to the tomb when the sun had risen" (Mark, 16, 1–2).

Von Stockhausen's way of depicting this scene departs from the traditional manner. The precise composition of the figures is reminiscent of medieval manuscript illuminations; the three women in particular seem to have only a vague connection with each other; their stiff attitudes indicate the tenseness of the situation. There is a tree in the corner at the bottom to the left and a faint suggestion of the grave; but all the four figures in the picture stand in what is an almost entirely abstract composition. It is mainly in the colours that the symbolic character of the scene is revealed: Mary Magdalene, Mary, and Salome walk upwards from the dark violet region of mourning and fear to the spot where victory over death and darkness is revealed in fiery, glaring colours.

Hans Gottfried von Stockhausen was born in 1920 at Trendelburg in Hesse, and now lives in Esslingen on the Neckar. He has produced a great many stained glass windows, amongst others some for the minster at Ulm and for churches at Luebeck, Dortmund, Bad Oeynhausen, and Hamburg.

The window reproduced here was made in the workshop of the *Hofkunstanstalt und Glasmalerei* of Franz Mayer at Munich.

56. *Sieburg, Benedictine Abbey of Michaelsberg. Ernst Jansen-Winkeln: Daniel in the den of lions*
57. *Kornelimünster, Benedictine Abbey. Ernst Jansen-Winkeln: The Crucifixion*

Both these windows were made in 1954 from designs by Ernst Jansen-Winkeln of Mönchen-Gladbach, at Linnich in the Rhineland in the workshop of the *Älteste Glasmalerei Deutschlands* of Dr. H. Oidtmann, who is well known in his own line for his book *Die rheinischen Glasmalereien vom 12. bis 16. Jahrhundert*, Düsseldorf, 1912 and 1929.

The picture of Daniel is a detail from the window at the side of the chancel in the Benedictine Abbey of Michaelsberg in Siegburg near Bonn; the Crucifixion is in the rosette of the window in the chancel of the Benedictine Abbey of Kornelimünster, which lies to the south-east of Aachen. Both pictures reveal a predilection for the medieval form of medallions for stained glass; modelling is replaced in these windows by a so-called expressionist drawing on the painting, showing interesting parallels with the art of Duelberg.

The expression of the group in the Crucifixion in its restrained style is almost as strong as that in Barlach's works.

58–59. *Munich, Liebfrauenkirche. Robert Rabolt: Statio Orbis 1960*

The Eucharistic World Congress held in Munich in 1960 has been impressively commemorated in the high window made by Robert Rabolt for the right-hand transept of the Liebfrauenkirche (Church of Our Lady). Of the three main panels of the centre band, each of which covers three tiers, those showing the Communion, the Last Supper, and the procession are reproduced here. In the upper part of the panel, called the *statio orbis*, there is a good representation of Holy Mass; Holy Communion is depicted together with the Last Supper, the horseshoe shape of the table obviously and symbolically their uniting force.

In the picture of the procession the solemn dynamic of the walking bishop and the cardinal is balanced by the poise of the worshipping figure. The picture succeeds in capturing an impression of the procession of the 1960 Eucharistic World Congress. The rich though on the whole cold colouring, the austere drawing, and the largely naïve and simple composition, show Rabolt to be an artist of great originality.

He was born in 1899 at Frankfort, and is now working at Munich. His main post-war works are church windows in Munich, Landau, Augsburg, Passau, Bremen, and Würzburg.

The stained glass reproduced here was made in the workshop of the *Hofkunstanstalt und Glasmalerei* of Franz Mayer at Munich.

60. *Aachen, Baptismal Chapel, Anton Wendling (1954)*

There are more important works by Professor Wendling than that reproduced here, but this particular one has been chosen because of its naturalistic symbolism and its strong bias towards abstract and ornamental art. The shoal of natural-looking white fish follows the *ichthys*, which is shown by the cross in its mouth to be Christ; the blue and the red fish, swimming past it, symbolise lukewarm Christians. Its rhythm and its symbolic force make this window very attractive.

Professor Anton Wendling was born in 1891 in Mönchen-Gladbach. He is one of the most important glass-painters of the Lower Rhine, where he has created various works of art, some geometrical and ornamental, others figurative in composition, showing an affinity of form to the art of Mataré. He made a mosaic for the papal pavilion at the World Exhibition in Brussels in 1937, and a mural painting for the Brussels Exhibition of 1958. Among his more important works are windows at Luxemburg, Cologne, Aachen, Juliers, Minden, Mainz, and Xanten.

The picture reproduced here dates from 1954; it was made in the workshop of the *Älteste Glasmalerei Deutschlands* of Dr. H. Oidtmann at Linnich in the Rhineland.

NOTES AND BIBLIOGRAPHY

1. HEINRICH GERHARD FRANZ: *Neue Funde zur Geschichte des Glasfensters*. In *Forschung und Fort-schritte. Nachrichtenblatt der deutschen Wissenschaft und Technik*, 29 (1955), 10.

   The same, *Die Stuckfenster in Qasr al-Hair al Gharbi*. This is a study of the window in the lunette, a motif of early Islamic art, of which not much notice has so far been taken. In *Wissenschaftkiche Annalen*, V (1956).

   D. C. BARAMKÉ: *Excavations at Khirbat al-Mafjar*, IV, QDAP, X (1942), XIV (1950): "When the winter palace at Khirbat al-Mafjar near Jericho was excavated, which dates from the time of the Umayyda Caliph Hisham, 724–743, fragments of unglazed stucco transennae were found, together with others with some glass set into them. This glass was of various colours, and on several pieces were black drawings in patterns resembling plants or geometrical figures."

2. The Abbey Church at Wissembourg was completed in 1070.

3. JEAN HUBERT: *Les origines de l'art français*, Paris, 1947, plate 149.

   JEAN-JACQUES GRUBER: *Technique*. In *Le vitrail français*, Paris, Edition des Deux Mondes, 1958, pp. 56–57, plate 35.

4. HANS WENTZEL: *Meisterwerke der Glasmalerei*, Berlin DVK, 1951, pp. 15–16, plate I, illustrations 1–6.

5. FRIDTJOF ZSCHOKKE: *Die romanischen Glasgemälde des Strassburger Münsters*, Basel, Benno Schwabe., 1942.

6. HANS WENTZEL: *Op. cit.*, illus. No. 137.

7. ROBERT BRUCK: *Die elsässische Glasmalerei, I–II*, Strassburg, 1902.

8. Eugen Heinen: *Dom und Kloster Altenberg*, Düsseldorf, ed. Hans Altenberg, 2nd ed., 1951, pp. 37–38, plates 20–21.
   Hans Wentzel: *Op. cit.*, plate 39.

9. Eva Frodl-Kraft: *Die mittelalterlichen Glasgemälde in Wien*. In *Corpus vitrearum medii aevi* (CVMA), Österreich I., Graz-Wien-Köln, Harmann Bohlaus Nachfolger, 1962.

10. With reference to architecture painted on stained glass, compare Eva Frodl-Kraft: *Architektur im Abbild. Ihre Spiegelung in der Glasmalerei*. In *Wiener Jahrbuch für Kunstgeschichte*, XVII.

11. Paul Frankl: *Peter Hemmel, Glasmaler von Andlau*, Berlin 1956. The same, *The obaldvon Lixheim*, in *Zeitschrift für Kunstwissenschaft*, XI (1957), pp. 55–90. He was an important glass-painter working at the end of the fifteenth and the beginning of the sixteenth centuries.

12. In particular the brothers Crabeth and Master Dirck in Gouda. Compare J. Helbig, *Die Glasschilderkunst in Belgie; Repertorien en Documenten*, 1943–1951. The same, *Meesterwerken van de Glasschilderkunst in de oude Nederlanden*, Antwerp, 1941.

13. Jean Lafond: *Le vitrail français de 1560 a 1789*. In *Le vitrail français*, note 3, illus. No. 208.

14. Hans Wentzel: *Die Glasmalerei der Zisterzienser in Deutschland*. In *L'architecture monastique. Actes et travaux de la recontre franco-allemande des historiens d'art, 1951. Die Klosterbaukunst. Arbeitsbericht der deutsch-französischen Kunsthistorikertagung (1951)*. Special number of the *Bulletin des relations artistiques France-Allemagne*, Mainz, May 1951.

15. Especially by using damask patterns on blue glass; previously festoons, lozenge-patterns and bull's-eye-patterns had been made to serve the same purpose.

16. Compare Hans Wentzel, *op. cit.*; illus. No. 238; Landsberg am Lech, St. Christopher, end of 15th century, and illus. No. 239, Munich, Salvator Church, St. Sebastian, about 1500, destroyed in 1945.

17. E. Panofsky: *Suger. On the Abbey Church of St. Denis and its Art Treasures*, Princeton, 1946.
    Louis Grodecki: *Vitraux de France du XIe au XVIe siècle*, Paris, 1953, pp. 38–40, Nos. 2–3.
    Louis Grodecki: *Les Vitraux allégoriques de Saint Denis*. In *Art de France*, 1961, pp. 19–46.

18. Louis Grodecki: *Op. cit., Le Mans*, pp. 40–41, No. 4.

19. Louis Grodecki: *Quelques observations sur le vitrail au XIIe siècle en Rhénanie et en France*. In *Mémorial du voyage en Rhénanie de le Société nationale des Antiquaires de France*, Paris 1953, pp. 2–41–4⁸.

20. Yves Delaporte and Etienne Houvet: *Les vitraux de la Cathédrale de Chartres*, Four vols. Chartres, 1926.

21. Marcel Aubret, Louis Grodecki, Jean Lafond, Jean Verrier: *Les vitraux de Notre-Dame et de la Sainte Chapelle*, CVMA, *France I*, Paris, 1959.

22. Ellen, J. Beer: *Die Rose der Kathedrale von Lausanne und der kosmologische Bilderkreis des Mittelalters*, Benteli, Bern, 1952.

23. Louis Grodecki: See note 17.

24. Louis Grodecki: *Les vitraux des églises de France*, Paris, 1947, p. 28.

25. Jean Lafond: in *Le vitrail français*.

26. P. E. Giusto: *Le vetrate di S. Francesco in Assisi*, Milan 1911.
   P. E. Kleinschmidt: *Die Basilika San Francesco in Assisi I*, Berlin, 1915.
   Hans Wentzel: *Die ältesten Farbfenster in der Oberkirche von San Francesco zu Assisi und die deutsche Glasmalerei des 13. Jahrhunderts*. In *Wallraf-Richarts-Jahrbuch XIV* (1952).

27. Giuseppe Marchini: *Le vitrail italien*, Milan, *Arts et Métiers graphiques*, 1955.

28. G. Poggi: *Le dôme de Florence*, Berlin, 1909.
   H. von Straelen: *Studien zur Florentiner Glasmalerei des Trecento und Quattrocento*, Wattenscheid, 1938.
   W. Paetz: *Die Kirchen von Florenz*, Frankfurt am Main, 1940–1953.
   P. Toesca: *Storia dell' arte italiana, II, Il Trecento*, Torino, 1951.

29. E. Carli: *Vetrato duccesca*, Florence, 1946.
   L. Fumi: *Il duomo di Orvieto*, Rome, 1891.

30. G. Marchini: *Op. cit.*, pp. 46–47, illus. No. XIV, plate 68.

31. C. L. Rogghianti: *Il Foppa e le vetriere del duomo di Milano*. In *Critica d'arte*, VI (1954).

32. C. Mancini: *Guglielmo de Marcillat*, Florence, 1909.

33. Joseph Ludwig Fischer: *Handbuch der Glasmalerei*, p. 83. Karl W. Hiersemann, Leipzig, 1914.

34. Herbert Read, John Baker, Alfred Lammer: English Stained Glass, London, Thames & Hudson, 1960.

35. Michael Stettler: *Königsfelden, Farbenfenster des 14. Jahrhunderts*, Laupen near Bern, 1949.
Emil Maurer: *Die Kunstdenkmäler des Kantons Aargau*, vol. III: *Das Kloster Königsfelden, Die Glasmalereien*, pp. 73–350.

36. Compare Robert Bruck, *op. cit.* Fritz Geiges: *Der mittelalterliche Fensterschmuck des Freiburger Münsters*, Freiburg in Breisgau, 1931.
Franz Kieslinger: *Gotische Glasmalerei in Österreich bis 1450*, Vienna, 1906.
Walter Frodl: *Glasmalerei in Kärnten 1150–1500*, Vienna, 1950.

37. Heinrich Oidtmann: *Die rheinischen Glasmalereien vom 12. bis zum 16. Jahrhundert*, Düsseldorf, I. 1912, II. 1929.
Hans Wentzel: *op. cit.*
Louis Grodecki: *Vidrieras romanicas*. In *Revista Goya*, 43/45, Madrid, 1961.

38. A. Galliner: *Glasgemälde des Mittelalters aus Wimpfen*, Freiburg, 1932.
Hans Wentzel: CVMA, *Deutschland I., Die Glasmalereien in Schwaben 1200–1350* (Esslingen.)
Mönchen-Gladbach: H. Oidtmann: *Op. cit.*
Franz Jansen: *Glasmalereien*. In *Kunstschätze der ehemaligen Benediktiner-Abtei Sankt Vitus*, Städtisches Museum, Ausstellung (Exhibition of City Museum), May-July 1948, Köln.
E. Schürer von Witzleben: *Die Glasfenster des Kölner Domes*. Aschaffenburg, N.D.

39. Hanns Swarzenski: *Die lateinischen illustrierten Handschriften des 13. Jahrhunderts in den Ländern am Rhein, Main und Donau*, Berlin, 1936.
Hans Wentzel: *Meisterwerke, op. cit.*
Victor Beyer: *Eine Strassburgische Glasmaler-Werkstätte des 13. Jahrhunderts und ihre Beziehungen zu den Rheinlanden*. In *Saarbrücker Hefte*, 4 (1956).
The same; *Les roses de réseau des bas-côtés de la cathédrale et l'oeuvre d'un atelier strasbourgeois du XIIIe siècle*. In *Bulletin de la Société des amis de cathédrale de Strasbourg*, 7 (1960).
Arthur Haseloff: *Eine thüringisch-sächsische Malerschule des 13. Jahrhunderts*, Strassburg, 1897.

40. Vienna: Eva Frodl-Kraft: CVMA, Österreich I, *op. cit.*
Erfurt: Margarete Bruckner and Ernst Hatge: *Der Zyklus der farbigen Glasfenster im Chor des Erfurter Domes.* In *Invent. Provinz Sachsen I.*, Burg, 1928.
H. Goern: *Die gotischen Bildfenster im Dom zu Erfurt*, Dresden, 1961.
Ulm: compare Hans Wentzel, *op cit.*

41. Eva Frodl-Kraft: CVMA, Österreich I, *op. cit.*

42. Viktring, F. Kieslinger: *op. cit.*—Walter Frodl, *op. cit.*
Eva Frodl-Kraft: CVMA, Österreich I.

43. Hans Wentzel: *Meisterwerke, op. cit.*

44. Setting: Dr. Hauck, in Saarbrücken, is preparing a study on the disks at Setting and their relation to the window in the chancel at Berne. For older literature compare Franc Xaver Kraus: *Kunst und Altertum in Elsass-Lothringen III, Lothringen*, pp. 926–934, illustrations 182–184.

45. Hans R. Hahnloser: *Chorfenster und Altäre des Berner Münsters*, Benteli, Bern-Bumplitz, 1950.

46. *Theophili Presbyteri et Monachi libri seu Diversarum Artium Schedula.*

47. The sharpness of the edge, necessary for the fixation of the grisaille painting, is, however, somewhat reduced when the disk is softened by the heat of the kiln.

48. One of the best examples of this technique is the disk with the head of Christ from Wissembourg, now in the Frauenhaus Museum at Strasbourg, though the strong lines of the face may have been touched up later on. For literature compare Louis Grodecki, *Vitraux de France du XIe au XVIe siècle.* In *Catalogue, mai-octobre 1953*, of *Musée des arts décoratifs*, Paris, pp. 37–38. Note also Wentzel, *op. cit.*

49. In his essay *Über Erhaltungszustand und Technik der Sakristeifenster von St. Gereon in Köln*, in *Jahrbuch der rheinischen Denkmalpflege*, XXII (1959, pp. 71–86. D. Rantsch of Bonn has shown that it was not patina that was applied on the outside, as has been widely assumed, but grisaille, used to increase the effect of the painting on the inside. Recently Dr. Frenzel of Nuremburg has also emphasized this fact, and given several examples of it.

50. The shape of the leads also varied in the course of the time. At first thick round leads were used, but later they were flatter with broader ends.

51. Even the removal of dirt, or the use of acids or alkalines can impair the restoration, and cause damage to any painting on the outside; see JEAN TARALON: *Le colloque international d'Erfurt et la sauvegarde des vitraux anciens*, in *Les monuments historiques de la France*, No. 4 (1962), pp. 231–246.

52. The Corpus vitrearum medii aevi works under the Comité international d'histoire de l'art. It is its task to take stock of all medieval stained glass, to treat it and to make reproductions of it.

CVMA = Corpus vitrearum medii aevi.
DVK   = Deutscher Verein für Kunstwissenschaft.
QDAP = Quarterly of the Department of Antiquities in Palestine.

Wissembourg (Alsace)

Augsburg Cathedral

Augsburg Cathedral

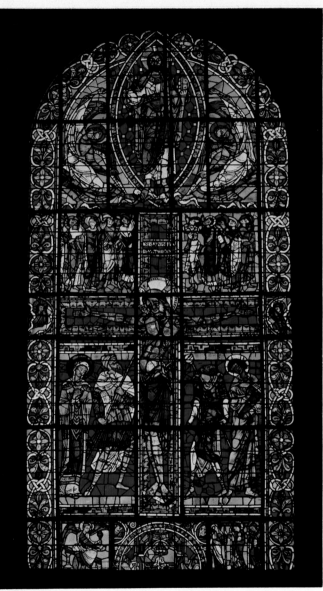

Poitiers Cathedral

4

Reims, Saint Rémi

Chartres: The Cathedral

6

Chartres: The Cathedral

Chartres: The Cathedral

Chartres: The Cathedral

9

Chartres: The Cathedral

Chartres: The Cathedral

Chartres: The Cathedral

Bourges: The Cathedral

Bourges: The Cathedral

Bourges: The Cathedral

Bourges: The Cathedral

Bourges: The Cathedral

Bourges: The Cathedral

18

Bourges: The Cathedral

19

Bourges: The Cathedral

Bourges: The Cathedral

Bourges: The Cathedral

Bourges: The Cathedral

Meissen Cathedral

Mönchen-Gladbach, The Abbey Church

Freiburg, Augustinian Museum

St. Florian, Augustinian Monastery

Cologne Cathedral

Cologne Cathedral

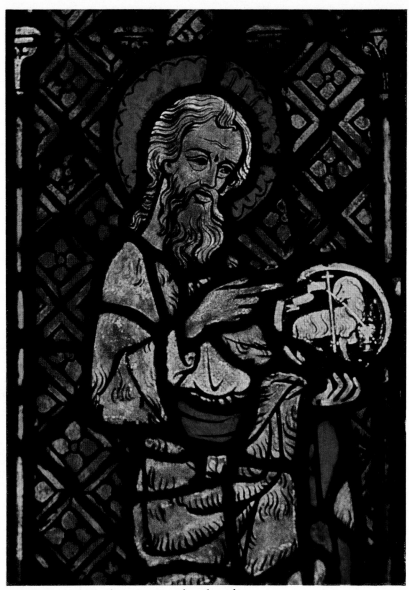

Cologne Cathedral : St. Mary's Chapel

Heiligkreuztal, Cistercian Abbey

31

Munich, Liebfrauenkirche

Strasbourg, Frauenhaus Museum

Herford, Johanneskirche

34

Herford, Johanneskirche

Königsfelden

Strasbourg, Frauenhaus Museum

Königsfelden

Königsfelden

39

Königsfelden

Königsfelden

Mulhouse, Stephanskirche

Viktring, Cistercian Abbey

Viktring, Cistercian Abbey

Viktring, Cistercian Abbey

45

Munich, Frauenkirche

Munich, Frauenkirche

St. Erhard in Styria, Parish Church

Munich, Frauenkirche

ave gracia plena dns tecum

Munich, Frauenkirche

50

Munich, Frauenkirche

Munich, Frauenkirche

Chaumont en Vexin, Parish Church

Private Collection, Nalini Jayasuriya, Ceylon

Private Collection, Hans Gottfried von Stockhausen

Ernst Jansen-Winkeln

Ernst Jansen Winkeln

Robert Rabolt

Robert Rabolt

Anton Wendling